FOCUS ON MEDIA BIAS

FOCUS ON MEDIA BIAS
BIAS IN REPORTING ON THE COVID-19 PANDEMIC

by Alex Gatling

FOCUS READERS.

VOYAGER

www.focusreaders.com

Copyright © 2022 by Focus Readers®, Lake Elmo, MN 55042. All rights reserved. No part of this book may be reproduced or utilized in any form or by any means without written permission from the publisher.

Focus Readers is distributed by North Star Editions:
sales@northstareditions.com | 888-417-0195

Produced for Focus Readers by Red Line Editorial.

Photographs ©: Shutterstock Images, cover, 1, 4–5, 14–15, 17, 19, 20–21, 23, 27, 28–29, 33, 34–35, 38, 45; Red Line Editorial, 7, 11; Patrick Semansky/AP Images, 8–9; Michael Brochstein/Sipa USA/AP Images, 13; Bill Feig/The Advocate/AP Images, 25; Yuri Gripas/Abaca/Sipa USA/AP Images, 31; Alex Brandon/AP Images, 37; Sue Ogrocki/AP Images, 40–41; Jacob Hamilton/Ann Arbor News/AP Images, 43

Library of Congress Cataloging-in-Publication Data
Library of Congress Cataloging-in-Publication Data is available on the Library of Congress website.

ISBN
978-1-64493-864-5 (hardcover)
978-1-64493-910-9 (paperback)
978-1-64493-996-3 (ebook pdf)
978-1-64493-956-7 (hosted ebook)

Printed in the United States of America
Mankato, MN
082021

ABOUT THE AUTHOR

Alex Gatling is a children's book writer from Texas. She enjoys traveling, learning about science and history, and staying informed on current events.

TABLE OF CONTENTS

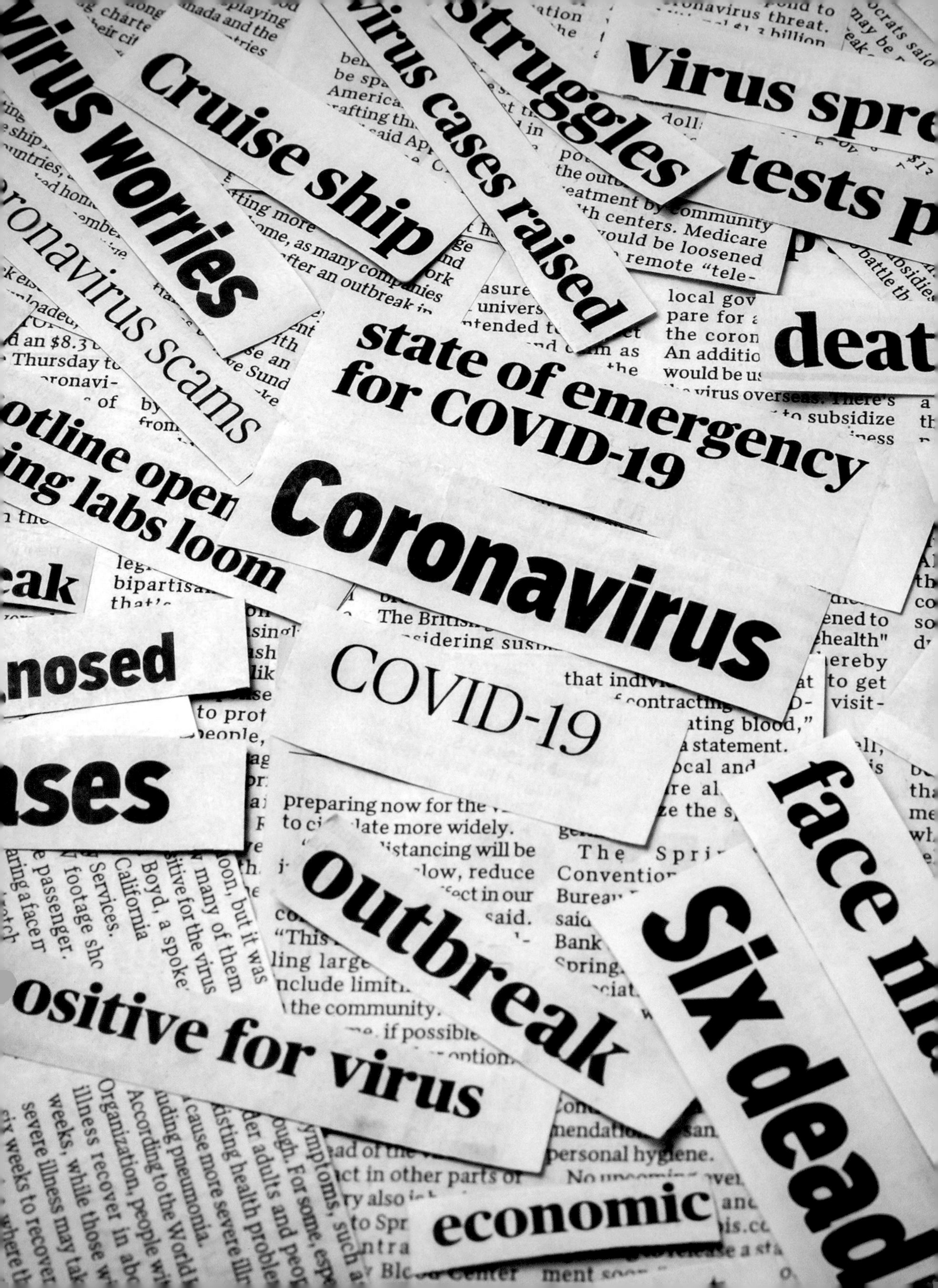
virus worries
Cruise ship
virus cases raised
struggles
Virus spre
tests p
Coronavirus scams
deat
state of emergency
for COVID-19
Coronavirus
otline open
ing labs loom
eak
nosed
COVID-19
ases
face
outbreak
Six dead
ositive for virus
economic

ONE STORY, TWO WAYS

On March 13, 2020, US President Donald Trump declared a national emergency. He was responding to the COVID-19 **pandemic**. News media reported on the story. These reports included both facts and **bias**.

Fox News is the largest TV news network in the United States. CNN is the second largest. Both news outlets also have articles online. And both websites reported on Trump's announcement.

The COVID-19 pandemic dominated the news in March 2020.

The Fox News article focused on the government's plan to work with US companies. The article said these companies would greatly increase testing for the virus. It also mentioned Trump's belief that the crisis would pass.

In contrast, the CNN article focused on government failures early in the pandemic. It said Trump refused to take responsibility for those failures. And it expressed doubts about the government's plan to increase testing. CNN and Fox News both reported on the same story. However, they gave very different messages to their readers.

COVID-19 spread quickly around the world. Huge amounts of information spread with it. The World Health Organization (WHO) called it an "infodemic." Some of the information was factual. But some was not. People sometimes shared information without **verifying** it. As a result, false information spread.

During the crisis, people struggled to find reliable information. They could not always tell true and false information apart. Overall, the infodemic increased people's fear. It also led some people to behave in unsafe ways.

STOPPING AN INFODEMIC ◄

As the red lines show, false information can spread quickly in an infodemic. Here are some ways to stop the spread.

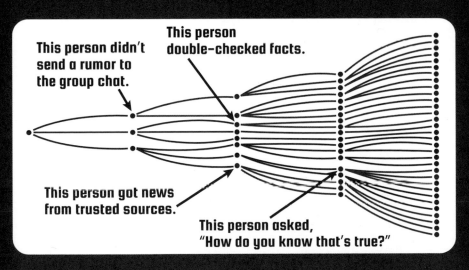

This person didn't send a rumor to the group chat.

This person double-checked facts.

This person got news from trusted sources.

This person asked, "How do you know that's true?"

CHAPTER 2

PANDEMIC COVERAGE

In early 2020, US news media did not focus much on COVID-19. Some articles mentioned a distant virus in Wuhan, China. But the media mostly focused on other events. Then COVID-19 came to the United States. By mid-March, COVID-19 news had overtaken all other news.

News media discussed the virus from many angles. COVID-19 was a health issue, of course. But politics and business articles also discussed

In January 2020, the US news media focused heavily on politics rather than COVID-19.

the virus. Entertainment and sports stories did, too. News media also focused on how the pandemic affected the economy.

Governments offered health messages to slow the virus's spread. These messages aimed to change people's behavior. People needed to know how to keep themselves and others safe. The media played a key role in sharing this information. For example, news media talked about physical distancing and mask-wearing. These actions helped slow the spread of the virus.

The data on COVID-19 changed quickly. In many cases, news media struggled to keep up.

> # ➤ THINK ABOUT IT

News coverage of COVID-19 changed over time. How does news coverage have an effect on what people care about?

Their readers and viewers did, too. News media did not always get the facts right on COVID-19. They did not always explain the science correctly. And they sometimes helped spread false information. Many Americans said they found it difficult to tell facts from made-up news.

US NEWS COVERAGE ◅

As the virus spread, US news coverage shifted its focus. These charts show the topics that received the most coverage during specific weeks of 2020.

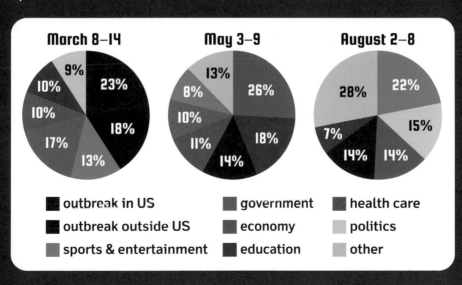

March 8–14
9%
10%
10%
17%
13%
18%
23%

May 3–9
13%
8%
10%
11%
14%
18%
26%

August 2–8
28%
22%
15%
7%
14%
14%

■ outbreak in US
■ outbreak outside US
■ sports & entertainment
■ government
■ economy
■ education
■ health care
■ politics
■ other

ANTI-ASIAN BIAS

The virus first appeared in China. Health experts called the virus SARS-CoV-2. The WHO called the disease that the virus caused COVID-19. These names were chosen on purpose. Experts did not want to connect the disease to a specific place or group of people.

However, certain US political leaders referred to it as the "Chinese virus." **Conservative** media used this language as well. The phrase affected many people's feelings about the virus. Some people blamed China for the virus. They associated the virus with Asian people. As a result, many Asian Americans experienced an increase in **racism**. And more non-Asian people committed crimes against Asian Americans.

Not all news media used the term "Chinese virus." Some news media said the phrase was racist. But even that coverage could have negative

▲ Anti-Asian bias increased after conservative talk show hosts such as Laura Ingraham blamed China for the virus.

results. Media experts argue that describing bias can indirectly increase it. Repeating ideas, even to criticize them, can spread those ideas. So, experts called on news media to be more thoughtful. They said reporters should stop repeating biased ideas. For example, reporters could stop using words or pictures that linked Asian people to the virus. Experts reminded reporters that language is powerful. The words people use matter.

CHAPTER 3

GETTING THE FACTS STRAIGHT

Several factors made it hard for people to find good information about COVID-19 in 2020. First, the virus was new. As a result, scientists didn't have much information about it. When scientists do research, they gain new data. Sometimes, the new data shows that old ideas were mistaken. So, scientists correct those conclusions. COVID-19 data changed as scientists did more research. Normally, this

Research can bring new information to light, and that can change what scientists believe about a topic.

process happens out of public view. Scientists do research over long periods of time. They wait until their research has been verified. Only then do they share their research with the public. But research happened faster during the pandemic. Sometimes news media reported on research that hadn't been verified. And sometimes scientists changed their ideas as they learned more. For some people, this changing information felt confusing or unreliable.

Also, many reporters who covered the virus did not have any health training. Without this training, they struggled to report **critically** on the research. Instead, many reporters tried to provide balance. Balance is a key standard of journalism. It means

➤ THINK ABOUT IT

When is balanced reporting useful and appropriate? When might it be a problem?

△ When reporters do not have health training, they may unintentionally spread misleading information.

reporters give equal time to different views. Balance typically helps people better understand a topic. But during the pandemic, this approach was misleading. Scientists were mostly in agreement on virus research. However, reporters sometimes spread unverified data in order to seem balanced.

Reporters often focus on what political leaders say. Sometimes, leaders make false claims. Often, news media still report what these leaders say. In doing so, news media help spread false ideas.

This situation happened frequently during the pandemic. For example, scientists studied one drug as a possible treatment. The study seemed to show positive results. Some political leaders talked to the media about the drug. But further research suggested the drug was not helpful. And some scientists said there were problems with the original study. Even so, political leaders continued to talk about the drug as a treatment. And news media reported what those leaders said. As a result, many people believed the drug worked.

Researchers criticized news media for simply reporting what political leaders said. They argued that news media should verify political leaders'

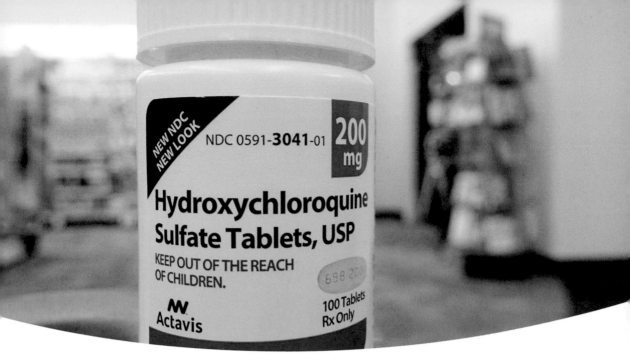

▲ A drug called hydroxychloroquine received heavy media coverage, but it was not effective against COVID-19.

claims. They should correct any incorrect claims right away. And they should focus more on the ideas of health experts.

News media did publish fact-checking reports. These reports corrected false claims about the pandemic. But these reports often came out later, after the claims had already begun to spread. And many articles spread false ideas without correction.

CHAPTER 4

FRAMING THE STORY

News framing shapes how people feel about current events. Reporters frame the news by choosing which topics to cover. They also choose how to present those topics.

News media framed the pandemic in a variety of ways. For example, some media presented the virus as a threat. Other media said the virus was not serious. Some media focused on how people could slow the virus's spread. Other media

When many different media outlets cover a story, the public tends to believe the story is important.

focused on how the pandemic was harming the economy. Some media described mask-wearing as a behavior that helped slow the spread. Other media said mask requirements limited people's freedom.

News framing shaped people's thoughts about the pandemic. And those thoughts influenced people's behaviors. Different messages led people to take different actions. For example, some people followed behaviors that slowed the virus's spread. Others protested against those behaviors.

US news media were consistent in one framing choice. They all framed the pandemic as negative. This framing might not be surprising. After all, how could pandemic news be positive? However, positive trends did happen during the pandemic. At times, the number of COVID-19 cases dropped. Schools reopened. Students returned to in-person

▲ US news media outperformed non-US news media in discussing the benefits of physical distancing and wearing masks.

lessons. And scientists made progress on creating vaccines.

Still, US news coverage was largely negative. For example, news outlets reported when COVID-19 cases increased. Reporters also wrote thousands of negative articles on US political leaders. These articles discussed leaders' false claims about the pandemic. And they mentioned when leaders did not follow safe behaviors.

Many fewer reports mentioned progress toward vaccine creation. Even US articles about vaccines showed negative bias. For example, British news media discussed how a vaccine could be created quickly. But US reports emphasized why a quick timeline might not be possible.

Researchers have long recognized a negativity bias in humans. People are more likely to pay attention to and remember negative events. This bias can be helpful. People try to learn from negative events. They try to prevent those events from happening again. But this bias can also drive negative news coverage. People pay more attention to negative stories. Researchers

➤ **THINK ABOUT IT**

What COVID-19 news stories do you remember? How did those stories make you feel?

△ More than 90 percent of US media coverage of COVID-19 was negative.

confirmed this bias with COVID-19 articles. The most popular US articles were also some of the most negative. So, US news media could have been responding to people's demand for negative news.

All this negativity had a cost. The number of US adults with signs of **depression** increased during the pandemic.

GENDER IMBALANCE

Many media sources showed bias in who they interviewed. Overall, women were far less represented than men. Women were typically presented as COVID-19 victims. Or they were treated as sources of personal opinion. Meanwhile, men were more likely to be interviewed as experts.

The gender gap went further. Most news reporters are men. But studies found that female reporters' articles on COVID-19 were more **credible**. On average, their reports went deeper into the topic. And their reports gave more information. Even so, men's voices dominated pandemic news coverage.

This imbalance had consequences. Women had little control over how the crisis was framed. And they had little influence over policy decisions.

Around the world, women provided 70 percent of health care. Yet they were less able to get care

▲ Women made up a minority of reporters, but they tended to write better articles about the pandemic.

themselves. More women than men left their jobs during the pandemic. They stayed home to care for their children. Some were unlikely to return to work. These factors especially affected women of color.

CHAPTER 5

ENDLESS NEWS CYCLE

A news cycle is the period of time that news media cover a particular story. Some stories are less interesting to the public than others. These stories do not have long news cycles. News media soon replace them with other stories. Meanwhile, the news cycles for major events often last much longer.

The news cycle for the pandemic was endless. News media continually discussed COVID-19.

During the pandemic, many people lost sleep because they were frequently checking the news.

On the one hand, the constant news coverage was useful. It helped people feel they had the knowledge they needed to keep themselves safe. For example, news coverage informed them of ways they could help slow the spread of the virus.

On the other hand, the constant news coverage was overwhelming. It caused many people to feel distress. Conflicting messages about COVID-19 increased this distress. Sometimes, health experts said one thing about the virus. Political leaders said another. News media spread both messages. People didn't always know who to trust.

This distress had negative effects. It led some people to stock up on certain supplies. For instance, people emptied stores of toilet paper and hand sanitizer. They also bought lots of face masks, leaving few available for health care workers. This panic-buying led to shortages.

Most stores were sold out of toilet paper during the first few weeks of the pandemic.

Distress caused some people to seek out health care they didn't need. People with mild illnesses filled clinics. They prevented truly sick people from getting the care they needed.

People also tried unsafe behaviors. News about miracle cures for COVID-19 spread on social media. Many of these so-called cures were actually dangerous. In Iran, one "cure" led to the deaths of hundreds of people.

Finally, distress led some people to avoid the news. Many Americans said that following COVID-19 news left them feeling worse. Taking breaks could be good for people's mental health. But it also meant they could miss important information. And they could forget how serious the crisis was. Researchers found that avoiding COVID-19 news had these negative effects. News avoidance was linked to people not practicing safe behaviors.

News coverage sometimes affected governments as well. Governments around the world had to respond to the pandemic. In some cases, news media got in the way of their plans. For example, the Italian government planned to put one area under lockdown. The people there would not be able to leave or move around. The goal was to keep people from spreading the virus.

◣ Many people read more news during the pandemic than they had done before. This often led to stress.

CNN learned about this plan. It reported the plan hours before the Italian government did. Many Italians reacted to the news. They wanted to leave the area before it went under lockdown. So, they filled airports and trains. These actions might have increased the virus's spread.

CHAPTER 6

PARTISAN BIAS

During the pandemic, the world's political leaders chose between different priorities. Some focused on the short-term economy. Others focused on plans to slow the virus's spread. Countries that focused on public health prevented many deaths. They also helped their economies in the long term. But these plans had negative effects in the short term. Many businesses closed. And many workers lost their jobs.

Movie theaters, restaurants, and many other businesses closed during the pandemic to keep people safe.

Conservatives and **liberals** have different values. Conservative and liberal news media show these differences, too. This bias shaped how news media talked about the risks of COVID-19. And it influenced how they discussed preventive behaviors. These are behaviors that helped people avoid getting and spreading the virus.

CNN is a liberal news channel. Fox News is a conservative news channel. Many studies compared their coverage of the pandemic. CNN's coverage remained mostly consistent. It followed the messages of health experts. In contrast, Fox News's coverage changed during the pandemic. In early 2020, the channel did not present COVID-19 as a serious threat. **Commentators** described the virus as a hoax. They said other news media were creating unnecessary panic. And they falsely described the disease as no worse than the flu.

Health experts such as Anthony Fauci received more coverage on CNN than on Fox News.

Fox News changed its coverage in mid-March. At that time, President Trump said the pandemic was a national emergency. Fox News began calling COVID-19 a "crisis." It encouraged people to practice physical distancing. In April and May, the channel's coverage changed again. Fox News

▲ The news media's coverage of the pandemic affected voters' opinions of the 2020 presidential candidates.

questioned if distancing was helpful. It framed the pandemic as not very serious. And it focused on the pandemic's negative economic effects.

The pandemic began during a US election year. Donald Trump, a Republican, was trying to win re-election. Joe Biden, a Democrat, was trying to take his place. Some researchers argued that conservative media were biased. They said these news sources tried to make Trump look good. For example, conservative media described Trump's pandemic response as positive. In contrast, liberal media tended to be critical of him. And both sides influenced how people voted.

Biased news coverage caused several problems in 2020. In particular, reports of false information contributed to the infodemic. These reports caused many people to believe untrue things. Researchers studied different news media and what their users believed about COVID-19. They found a clear link. Users of different news media had different views on the pandemic. They had different beliefs about how dangerous the virus was. They also disagreed on how to stay safe. Those beliefs affected people's actions. And those actions affected how fast the virus spread.

CHAPTER 7

MAKING DECISIONS

Past studies found that biased news can lead people to ignore the advice of scientists. Those studies focused on the issues of climate change and vaccination. During the COVID-19 pandemic, researchers did similar studies. They looked at people's behavior. And they studied people's media choices. They wanted to see if there was a link between the two. There was. Researchers compared viewers of Fox News

People who used conservative news sources were more likely to take risky actions, such as gathering in large groups.

and CNN. They looked at both risky actions and preventive actions. Risky actions included going to events with more than 10 people. Preventive actions included wearing masks and washing hands often. Researchers found that Fox News viewers took more risky actions. CNN viewers took more preventive actions.

Researchers couldn't determine if different news media actually caused people to behave differently. All they found was a link between news media and people's behaviors. And there could be many reasons for that link.

For example, liberal areas had higher levels of COVID-19 at the start of the pandemic. They saw more illnesses and deaths. So, people in those areas may have seen COVID-19 as a threat. That belief might have led them to practice more safe behaviors. People in liberal areas are more

▲ People who used liberal news sources were more likely to engage in safe behaviors, such as physical distancing.

likely to watch CNN than Fox News. But that news media choice only **correlated** with their actions. It didn't necessarily cause those actions.

People often follow media that agrees with what they already believe. This is called confirmation bias. People trust the facts that agree with their beliefs. And they often ignore facts that disagree with their beliefs. Studies also show that people value their own opinions over the advice of experts. This is especially true when experts advise people to do things they don't want to do. People tend to just do what they want.

For example, conservatives tend to value personal freedom. This value can sometimes be at odds with public health. During the pandemic, some state governments required people to wear masks. Many conservatives felt this requirement limited their freedom. They chose not to wear masks. Conservatives are more likely to watch Fox News than CNN. But watching Fox News didn't necessarily cause them not to wear masks.

> ## THINK ABOUT IT

Can you think of ideas that you are biased toward? How can people work to overcome confirmation bias?

By the summer of 2021, at least 600,000 Americans had died from COVID-19.

People choose which news media to consume. The media they choose often confirms their beliefs. News media also help shape what people think. In particular, news media play an important role during a crisis. They share information. That information can help determine what actions people will take to protect themselves and others.

BIAS IN REPORTING ON THE COVID-19 PANDEMIC

Write your answers on a separate piece of paper.

1. Write a paragraph explaining the main ideas of Chapter 3.

2. What responsibility do you think news media have during a crisis?

3. What is the term for a huge amount of information that spreads quickly?

    A. pandemic

    B. news cycle

    C. infodemic

4. Which is an example of confirmation bias?

    A. news media presenting the pandemic in a negative way

    B. people choosing news sources that agree with what they already believe

    C. political leaders using the term "Chinese virus"

Answer key on page 48.

GLOSSARY

bias
An attitude that causes someone to treat certain ideas unfairly.

commentators
People on news channels or news websites who give their opinions
on current events.

conservative
Supporting traditional views or values, often resisting changes.

correlated
Had a connection with something but did not necessarily cause that
thing to happen.

credible
Trustworthy and reliable.

critically
In a way that uses logic and facts to test ideas.

depression
A medical condition of deep, long-lasting sadness or loss
of interest.

liberals
People who support changes to traditional views or values.

pandemic
A disease that spreads quickly around the world.

racism
Hatred or mistreatment of people because of their skin color or
ethnicity.

verifying
Making sure that something is true and has no mistakes.

TO LEARN MORE

BOOKS

Doeden, Matt. *The COVID-19 Pandemic: A Coronavirus Timeline*. Minneapolis: Lerner Publications, 2021.

Gresko, Marcia S. *COVID-19 and the Challenges of the New Normal*. San Diego: ReferencePoint Press, 2021.

Hustad, Douglas. *Understanding COVID-19*. Minneapolis: Abdo Publishing, 2021.

NOTE TO EDUCATORS

Visit **www.focusreaders.com** to find lesson plans, activities, links, and other resources related to this title.

INDEX

Answer Key: 1. Answers will vary; 2. Answers will vary; 3. C; 4. B